Get to Work with Science and Technology

Asteroid Hunters

by Ruth Owen

Consultant:

Kevin Yates
Fellow of the Royal Astronomical Society

Ruby Tuesday Books

Published in 2016 by Ruby Tuesday Books Ltd.

Editor: Mark J. Sachner
Designer: Emma Randall
Production: John Lingham

Photo Credits:
Alamy: 22; Corbis: 12; Cosmographics: 23 (top); ESA: 13 (bottom); ESO: 10, 11 (bottom); Istock Photo: Cover, 14; Martin Mobberley: 13 (top); NASA: 4, 19 (bottom), 26, 27, 28–29; Rob Ratkowski/ Pan-STARRS: 9 (top), 14; Ruby Tuesday Books: 8, 15, 17 (bottom), 18, 19 (top), 24, 25, 30; Science Photo Library: 11 (top), 20, 21 (top); Shutterstock: Cover, 4 (bottom), 5, 6–7, 14, 17, 23 (bottom), 30; Karen Teramura: 9 (bottom); Wikipedia Creative Commons: 16, 21 (bottom).

Library of Congress Control Number: 2015907063

ISBN 978-1-910549-36-0

Printed and published in the United States of America

For further information including rights and permissions requests, please contact our Customer Service Department at 877-337-8577.

Contents

A Date with Disaster

It was June 2004. At a mountaintop **observatory** in Arizona, three **asteroid** hunters were studying grainy images captured by a **telescope**. As the scientists stared at a computer screen, they knew they had made an exciting discovery—a new asteroid! Using telescopes, they tried to see more of the asteroid, but it disappeared from view.

The white dot in this image is the newly discovered asteroid.

Scientists used a telescope at the Kitt Peak Observatory in Arizona to discover the asteroid.

There is a telescope inside this building.

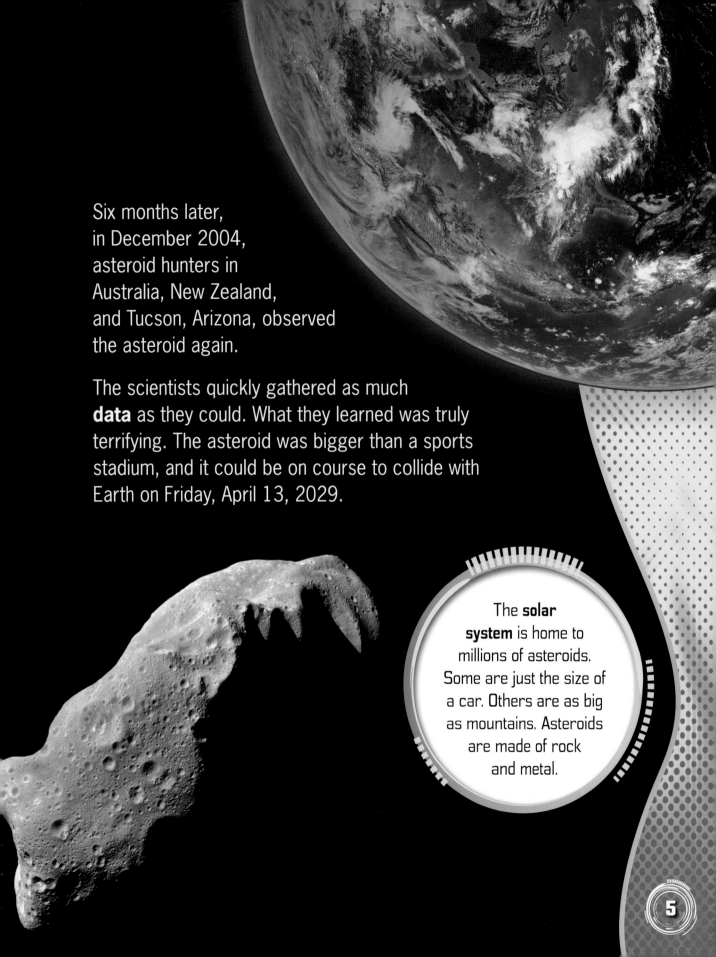

Six months later, in December 2004, asteroid hunters in Australia, New Zealand, and Tucson, Arizona, observed the asteroid again.

The scientists quickly gathered as much **data** as they could. What they learned was truly terrifying. The asteroid was bigger than a sports stadium, and it could be on course to collide with Earth on Friday, April 13, 2029.

The **solar system** is home to millions of asteroids. Some are just the size of a car. Others are as big as mountains. Asteroids are made of rock and metal.

A Threat from Outer Space?

What could happen if the newly discovered asteroid collided with Earth?

As it plunged through Earth's **atmosphere**, the asteroid would become a mountain-sized fireball. At the impact point with Earth, it would create a deep **crater** 2.7 miles (4.3 km) wide. For miles around the impact, bridges and buildings would collapse. The area where the asteroid hit would suffer utter devastation. Even 1,200 miles (1,931 km) from the impact, people would hear the blast.

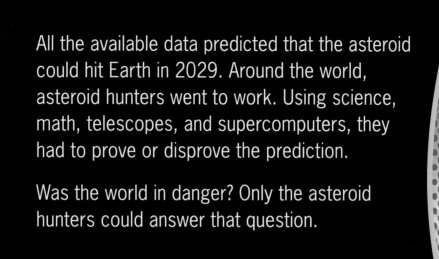

All the available data predicted that the asteroid could hit Earth in 2029. Around the world, asteroid hunters went to work. Using science, math, telescopes, and supercomputers, they had to prove or disprove the prediction.

Was the world in danger? Only the asteroid hunters could answer that question.

The new asteroid was discovered by asteroid hunters David J. Tholen, Roy A. Tucker, and Fabrizio Bernardi. They named it Apophis after a character in the TV show *Stargate*. Apophis was also the ancient Egyptian god of evil, darkness, and destruction.

Travelers of the Solar System

Just like Earth, asteroids **orbit**, or circle, the Sun. Each asteroid travels through space on its own pathway. Most asteroids in the solar system are circling between the orbits of Mars and Jupiter. They form a vast donut-shaped ring known as the asteroid belt. Some asteroids, however, hurtle through space on journeys that bring them into Earth's neighborhood.

Asteroids and **comets** that come close to Earth's orbit are known as Near Earth Objects (NEOs). Asteroids that come close to Earth's orbit are also known as Near Earth Asteroids (NEAs).

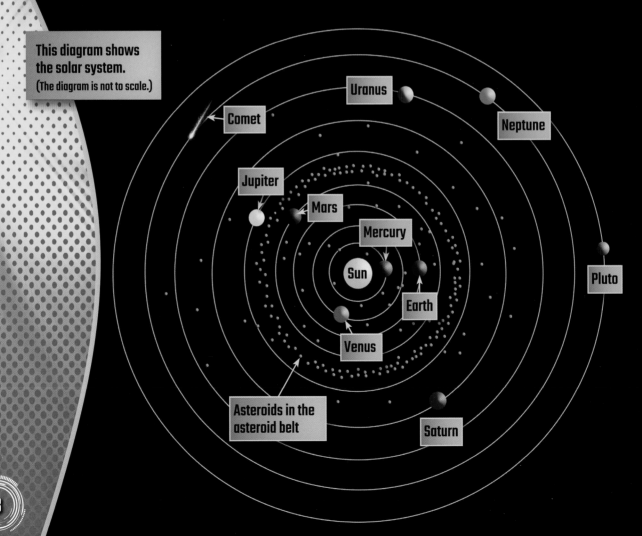

This diagram shows the solar system.
(The diagram is not to scale.)

Uranus

Comet

Neptune

Jupiter

Mars

Mercury

Sun

Pluto

Earth

Venus

Asteroids in the asteroid belt

Saturn

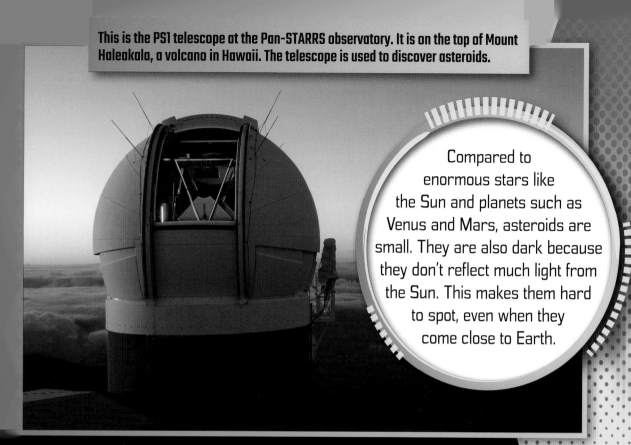

This is the PS1 telescope at the Pan-STARRS observatory. It is on the top of Mount Haleakala, a volcano in Hawaii. The telescope is used to discover asteroids.

Compared to enormous stars like the Sun and planets such as Venus and Mars, asteroids are small. They are also dark because they don't reflect much light from the Sun. This makes them hard to spot, even when they come close to Earth.

Asteroid hunters Richard Wainscoat (left) and Marco Micheli

The white dot on the computer screen is a Near Earth Asteroid discovered by the PS1 telescope.

So how near is near? NEOs are objects that come within 28 million miles (45 million km) of Earth's orbit. That may not sound very close, but in the vastness of space, it's a tiny distance.

Who Are the Asteroid Hunters?

Asteroid hunters are **astronomers**, or space scientists, with a passion for finding and studying asteroids and comets. Some asteroid hunters are amateurs. This means they watch for asteroids as a hobby. Others do it as their job.

Asteroid hunters work at observatories, usually at night. The best views of the sky are found away from city lights and in high places where the atmosphere is thinner. So many observatories are on mountaintops in remote places such as deserts.

Asteroid hunters don't only search for asteroids. They may also study planets, moons, and stars. Sometimes, they help design, build, or repair telescopes.

The Paranal Observatory in the Atacama Desert in Chile

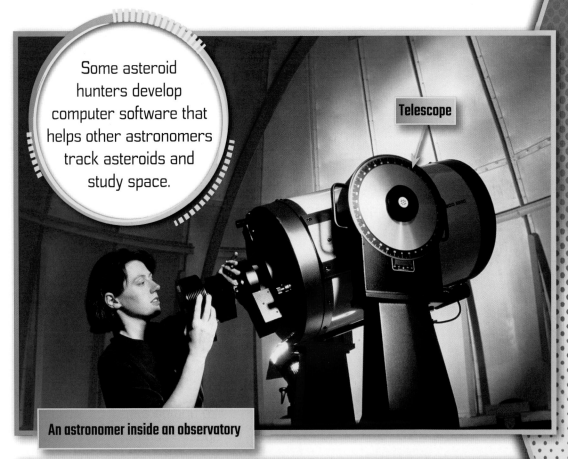

Some asteroid hunters develop computer software that helps other astronomers track asteroids and study space.

Telescope

An astronomer inside an observatory

The Vista telescope at the Paranal Observatory

Searching the Skies

To search for asteroids, an astronomer programs a telescope to observe a particular area in the sky. Everything the telescope sees is captured as a digital image by a camera that's connected to the telescope. Then the astronomer carefully checks the images to look for asteroids. In a single year, an astronomer might study more than 100,000 images of space!

When an asteroid is first spotted, its coordinates, or position in the sky, are calculated. Just like finding a spot on a map, special computer software pinpoints where in the sky the asteroid was first seen.

An astronomer checking images on a computer that's connected to his telescope

Most asteroids are discovered by huge, powerful telescopes. These telescopes are programmed to watch vast areas of the sky. The images captured by these telescopes are analyzed by computers that scan the pictures for asteroids. Teams of astronomers at observatories take care of these telescopes and keep watch over the computer results.

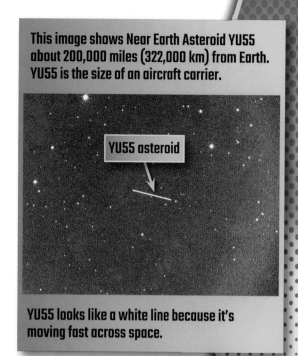

This image shows Near Earth Asteroid YU55 about 200,000 miles (322,000 km) from Earth. YU55 is the size of an aircraft carrier.

YU55 asteroid

YU55 looks like a white line because it's moving fast across space.

The control room at an observatory

Asteroid Hunting with Supercomputers

When a new asteroid is discovered, the Minor Planet Center (MPC) in Cambridge Massachusetts, must be notified. Asteroid hunters send their measurements of an asteroid's position in the sky to MPC. The scientists at MPC add the asteroid to their database. The MPC's database shows all the known asteroids and comets in the solar system.

Large telescopes, such as the Pan-STARRS PS1 telescope, upload their data to the Minor Planet Center, computer to computer.

Next, the new asteroid's orbit must be predicted to discover if it's a danger to Earth. All the asteroid's data is uploaded to a supercomputer—**NASA**'s Sentry System. This powerful computer predicts the thousands, or possibly even millions, of different orbits the asteroid might be on. It immediately shows if any of the possible orbits put the asteroid on a collision course with Earth.

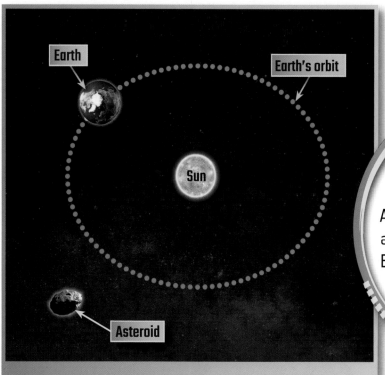

This diagram shows a newly discovered asteroid. Where is it heading?
(The diagram is not to scale.)

Every asteroid is given a number from zero to 10 on the Torino Scale. A Torino rating of zero means an asteroid is not a danger to Earth. A rating of 10 means a catastrophic collision with Earth is certain!

If an impact with Earth is predicted, it must then be proved or disproved. Each time an asteroid hunter observes the asteroid, its latest position is fed into the supercomputer. Just like piecing together a jigsaw puzzle, the asteroid's actual orbit becomes clear.

Hunting for Apophis

In June 2004, asteroid hunters discovered the asteroid Apophis. Then, on December 18, 2004, they spotted it again. These observations were uploaded to NASA's Sentry System.

The supercomputer's predictions showed that Apophis could collide with Earth on April 13, 2029. Was this prediction correct?

To answer that question, more observations were needed. Like detectives hunting for clues, asteroid hunters desperately watched the skies for Apophis. They also studied thousands of images of the sky from before the asteroid was discovered in June 2004.

Sometimes it is possible to photograph an object in space without knowing it. For example, an astronomer might be photographing stars and not looking for asteroids. Asteroid hunters can study old images of the sky to see if a newly discovered asteroid appears in these old photos.

The asteroid hunters who discovered Apophis in June 2004

Roy A. Tucker   David J. Tholen   Fabrizio Bernardi

Finally, astronomers Anne Descour and Jeff Larsen found something crucial—an older image of Apophis. The picture showed the asteroid's location in the sky back in March 2004. This new data was uploaded to Sentry.

Could this extra data help rule out the possible collision? Or would it still show that the giant asteroid might collide with Earth?

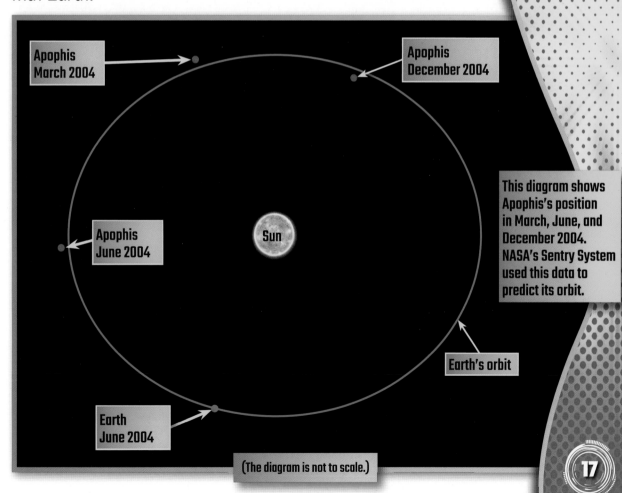

Apophis
March 2004

Apophis
December 2004

Apophis
June 2004

Sun

This diagram shows Apophis's position in March, June, and December 2004. NASA's Sentry System used this data to predict its orbit.

Earth's orbit

Earth
June 2004

(The diagram is not to scale.)

A Space Neighbor Drops By

The newly discovered data changed everything. Apophis would pass incredibly close to Earth. It would not, however, collide with our planet in 2029!

On April 13, 2029, Apophis will hurtle past Earth. It will fly just 19,400 miles (31,221 km) above the planet's surface. That's closer than the Moon. It's even closer than the **satellites** that give us TV and cell phone signals.

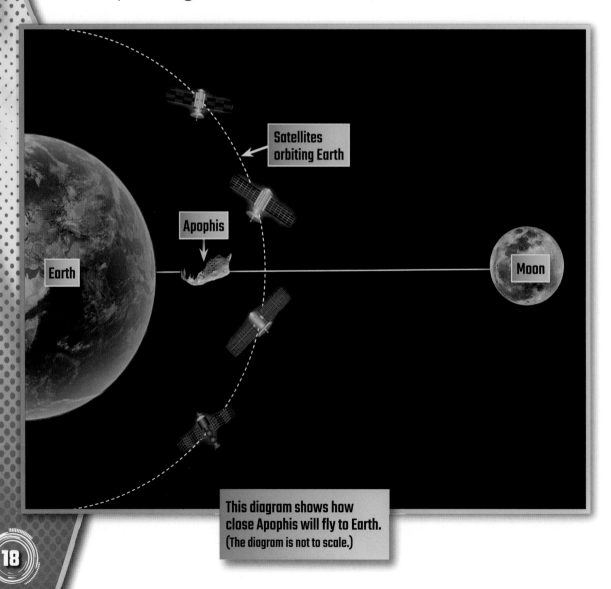

Satellites orbiting Earth

Apophis

Earth

Moon

This diagram shows how close Apophis will fly to Earth. (The diagram is not to scale.)

Since 2004, Apophis has been observed more than 4,000 times. It's been watched by asteroid hunters from Hawaii to Russia, and Spain to Japan. Each time it's spotted, more data is collected. Now scientists know that Apophis will not be a threat to Earth for at least the next 100 years.

Apophis is 1,066 feet (325 m) wide. Astronomers estimate that it weighs 67 million tons (61 million tonnes).

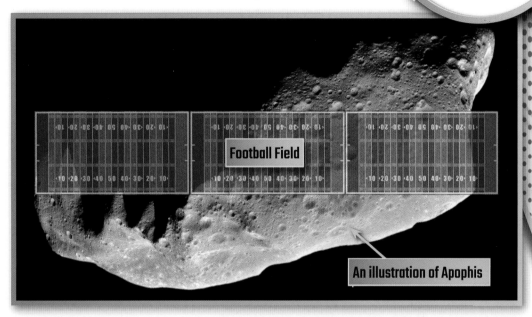

Football Field

An illustration of Apophis

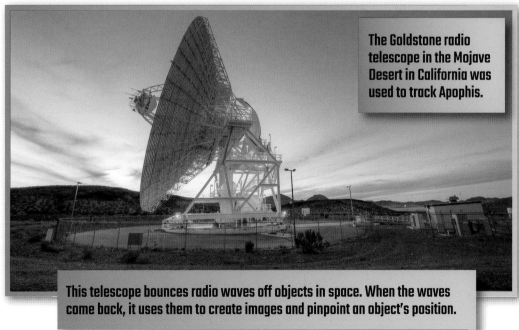

The Goldstone radio telescope in the Mojave Desert in California was used to track Apophis.

This telescope bounces radio waves off objects in space. When the waves come back, it uses them to create images and pinpoint an object's position.

Spaceguard in Action

The network of asteroid hunters who keep watch for Near Earth Objects (NEOs) is known as Spaceguard. On October 6, 2008, Spaceguard was put to the test.

On that day, asteroid hunter Richard Kowalski discovered a new NEO. It was given the number 2008 TC3. In just a few hours, asteroid hunters around the world made 500 observations of the object. NASA's supercomputer calculated that the NEO would collide with Earth the next day!

Near Earth Object 2008 TC3	
Size:	13.5 feet (4.1 m) wide
Weight:	88 tons (80 tonnes)
Speed:	29,000 mph (46,671 km/h)

Thankfully, the fast-moving object was heading for the remote Nubian Desert in Sudan, Africa. On October 7, it entered Earth's atmosphere and exploded in a fireball over the desert.

Spaceguard acted as an early warning system. If the NEO had been heading for a city, people could have been **evacuated**.

Meteorite

Dr. Peter Jenniskens (left) led the team that searched for meteorites from 2008 TC3.

Pieces of an asteroid that land on Earth are called **meteorites**. Scientists found 600 small, rocky meteorites from 2008 TC3 in the Nubian Desert. The meteorites were collected to be studied.

Earth Under Attack!

Has Earth ever been hit by a truly giant Near Earth Object?

About 65 million years ago, a massive asteroid or comet smashed into Earth. The object was about 6 miles (9.7 km) wide.

No one knows what happened that day, but scientists have many **theories**. The impact would have caused earthquakes, **tsunamis**, and fires.

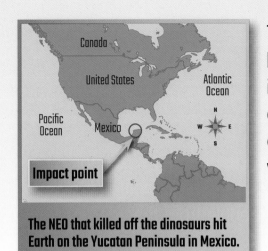

The NEO that killed off the dinosaurs hit Earth on the Yucatan Peninsula in Mexico.

The impact would also have blasted dust and ash into the sky that blocked out sunlight. Across the dark, burning land, plants would have died.

When Earth suffered this catastrophe, about 70 percent of all living things were wiped out—including the dinosaurs.

About 50,000 years ago, a huge metal asteroid smashed into Arizona. The asteroid created a crater that's about 1 mile (1.6 km) wide. It is known as Barringer Crater.

Barringer Crater

Defending Earth

What will we do if one day a giant asteroid is a threat to our planet?

The men and women of Spaceguard constantly keep watch for Near Earth Objects. Therefore, it's likely we will have plenty of warning. There will be time to evacuate people from the impact area.

If scientists had 10 or 20 years warning, a mission could be launched to change the asteroid's orbit. A robotic spacecraft known as a **gravity** tractor could fly alongside the asteroid. The spacecraft's gravity would gradually pull the asteroid off course so it misses Earth.

No one has designed or built a gravity tractor yet. This will be a project for scientists and **engineers** of the future.

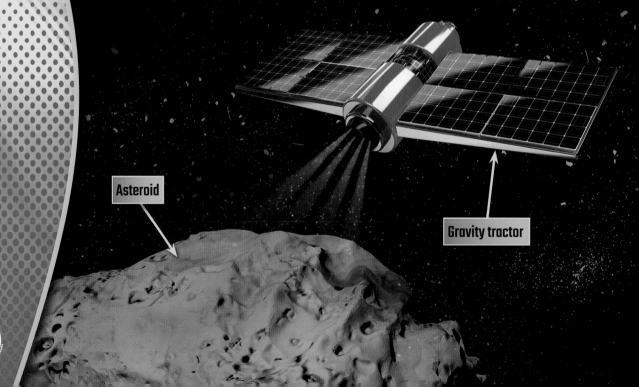

Asteroid

Gravity tractor

If a giant asteroid was on course to hit Earth, a nuclear weapon could be sent into space. The weapon would explode close to the asteroid. The blast would blow the asteroid off course and away from Earth.

A Mission to an Asteroid

One day, scientists may have to protect Earth from an asteroid. To do this, they need to know as much as possible about our rocky space neighbors.

In 2016, scientists will send a robotic spacecraft to an asteroid named Bennu. The *Osiris Rex* spacecraft will reach Bennu in 2018. The spacecraft will hover just above the surface of the asteroid. Then the "touch and go" robotic arm will take just five seconds to collect samples of loose rocks and soil.

The samples will be blasted back to Earth in a Sample Return Capsule. The capsule will land in the Utah desert in 2023. Then the *Osiris Rex* mission team will get to work studying the samples.

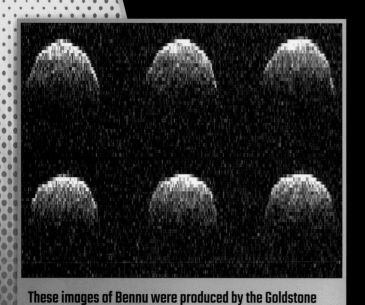

These images of Bennu were produced by the Goldstone radio telescope in California.

The asteroid Bennu may collide with Earth between the years 2175 and 2196. Knowing what it's made of could be very useful to future scientists if they need to knock it off course!

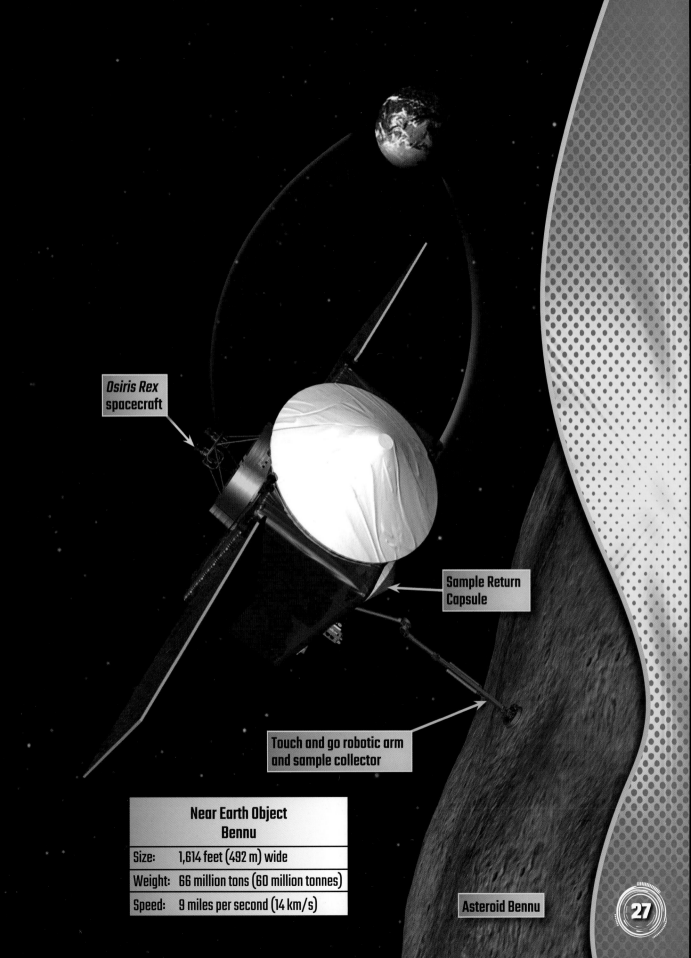

Osiris Rex
spacecraft

Sample Return
Capsule

Touch and go robotic arm
and sample collector

Near Earth Object Bennu	
Size:	1,614 feet (492 m) wide
Weight:	66 million tons (60 million tonnes)
Speed:	9 miles per second (14 km/s)

Asteroid Bennu

Asteroid Hunters on Guard

Every year, asteroid hunters discover more than 1,000 new Near Earth Asteroids. They also make millions of observations of asteroids. Every observation is uploaded to the Sentry System. This allows everyone in Spaceguard to keep track of new threats. They can also see if any known asteroids have changed course.

At this moment in time, scientists do not know of any asteroids that will threaten Earth in the next 100 years.

Every day, asteroid hunters keep watch over our solar system using technology and their science skills. They know their work must be careful and accurate. They cannot let down their guard for a moment.

One day, the future of our planet could depend on it!

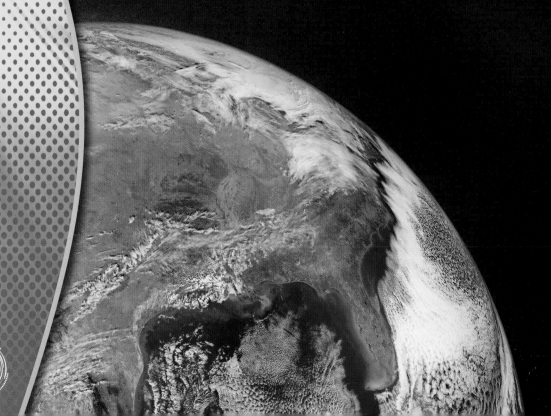

NEOWISE telescope

The NEOWISE (Near Earth Object Wide-field Infrared Survey Explorer) telescope orbits Earth searching for NEOs. It sees objects by how much heat they give off rather than how bright they are.

Amy Mainzer is the chief NASA scientist for the NEOWISE project.

Get to Work as an Asteroid Hunter

What subjects should I study to be an astronomer or asteroid hunter?
You will need to study and enjoy math and science subjects, such as physics and chemistry. At a college or university, you will study astronomy, physics, or space science, which is called astrophysics.

How soon can I get started?
Astronomy is a great hobby, so find out if there's an astronomy club at your school or go online to check out opportunities near you.

Where do astronomers and asteroid hunters work?
They work at observatories, universities, and science museums. Some get to work with space agencies such as NASA, CSA (Canadian Space Agency), or ESA (European Space Agency). Astronomers and asteroid hunters often get to travel all over the world.

When does an astronomer or asteroid hunter work?
There's work to be done day and night. Be prepared to work weekends, and even on holidays—something exciting could zoom into view at any time!

Crater Investigator

When a giant asteroid hits a planet or moon, the impact makes a crater. Investigate craters and how they form with this experiment.

How does the speed of an asteroid affect the size of the crater it makes?

Procedure:

1. Fill the baking dish with flour or sand. Smooth out the flour or sand so it's level and flat.
2. Hold the ball bearing 12 inches (30.5 cm) above the tray and then drop it.
3. Measure the diameter of the crater and record the data in your notebook. Then smooth out the flour or sand.
4. Repeat the experiment by dropping the ball bearing from the following heights: 24 inches (61 cm), 36 inches (91.4 cm), 48 inches (122 cm).

Materials:

- Large metal baking dish at least 3 inches (7.62 cm) deep
- Enough flour or sand to fill the baking dish
- A marble-sized steel ball bearing
- A measuring tape
- A notebook and pen

Questions:

1. What do you observe about the size of the craters as the drop height increases?
2. Does the ball bearing hit the flour or sand at the same speed when dropped from different heights?
3. What force do you think is making the ball bearing accelerate?

(The answers to these questions are on page 32.)

Visit the Sentry System

Just like asteroid hunters around the world, you can go online and look at NASA's Sentry System Risk Table.

Go to: **http://neo.jpl.nasa.gov/risks/**

Here you will find all the data on Near Earth Asteroids (NEAs) such as Apophis and Bennu.

Glossary

asteroid (AS-teh-royd)
A large rock or metal object that is orbiting the Sun.

astronomer (uh-STRAH-nuh-mer)
A scientist who specializes in the study of outer space.

atmosphere (AT-muh-sfeer)
A layer of gases around a planet, moon, or star.

comet (KAH-mit)
A space object made of ice, rock, and dust that is orbiting the Sun.

crater (KRAY-tur)
A bowl-shaped hole in the ground. Craters are usually caused by asteroids or comets hitting the surface of a planet or moon.

data (DAY-tuh)
Information and facts, often in the form of numbers.

engineer (en-juh-NIHR)
A person who uses math, science, and technology to design and build machines.

evacuated (ih-VAK-yoo-ate-id)
Moved quickly from a place of danger.

gravity (GRA-vuh-tee)
The force that causes objects to be pulled toward other objects.

meteorite (MEE-tee-uhr-ite)
A piece of an asteroid or other rocky object that has landed on a planet or moon.

NASA (NAS-ah)
A group of scientists and space experts in the United States. NASA studies space and builds spacecraft. The letters in NASA stand for "National Aeronautics and Space Administration."

observatory (uhb-ZUR-vuh-tor-ee)
A building or other structure that houses a telescope.

orbit (OR-bit)
To circle, or move around, another object.

satellite (SA-tih-lyt)
An object that orbits a planet or other object in space. A satellite may be natural, such as a moon, or made by people, such as the satellites used for transmitting TV and cell phone signals.

solar system (SOH-ler SIS-tem)
The Sun and all the objects that orbit it, such as planets, their moons, asteroids, and comets.

telescope (TEL-uh-scope)
A tool or machine used for viewing space.

theory (THIHR-ee)
An idea that tries to explain things that people observe.

tsunami (tsoo-NAH-mee)
A huge wave or group of waves often caused by an earthquake under the ocean.

Index

Read More

Owen, Ruth. *Astronomers (Out Of The Lab: Extreme Jobs in Science).* New York: Rosen Publishing (2014).

Portman, Michael. *Could an Asteroid Harm Earth? (Space Mysteries).* New York: Gareth Stevens Publishing (2013).

Learn More Online

To learn more about asteroid hunters and asteroids, go to:
www.rubytuesdaybooks.com/asteroidhunters

Answers Page 30

1) The size of the craters increases as the drop height increases.

2) As the drop height increases, the speed of the ball bearing on impact increases.

3) Gravity is making the ball bearing accelerate as it falls.